CONTENTS

GW00691275

03

LUCAS

Part of the Mirror Collection
© Published by Trinity Mirror
Images: Mirrorpix
Jenson Button cover image: PA Photos
Printed by PCP

SALUTE TO SILVERSTONE

RACING IN A SPEEDSTER IS WITHIN REACH NOW

"DAILY MIRROR" REPORTER

A MIDGET speedster costing about one-sixth of the price of a big racing car has brought a new sport within the reach of the ordinary man.

Motor racing previously was always expensive—a big racing car cost upwards of several thousand pounds.

A cheap car requiring little technical knowledge was what was wanted for the ordinary man.

So a group of enthusiasts in Bristol, in 1946, began to build midget speedsters round a 500 c.c. motor-cycle engine. The engine and gear-box, costing £40-£50, was the most expensive item.

They claim the final product should cost between £125 and £350.

The idea caught on, and young men with the not-so-deep pockets, but itching to get into motor racing, seized on it.

And so the "500" was evolved—a noisy, smelly, chain-driven baby, capable of getting along on a methyl-alcohol mixture at 100 m.p.h plus.

Professional builders took up the idea, and today the less technically skilled young men can buy a hand-built Cooper, Marwyn or Bond for between £445 and £800.

Export Demand

The movement has also been taken up abroad. British professionally-built models are in large demand for export to most of these countries.

In England the main centres for the midget racers are London, Bristol, Northampton and Leeds. More will be established this year, John Gale, secretary of the 500 Club, tells me.

"The '500' has now opened motor racing to an enormous new field," he says.

"More and more amateurs are being attracted and our great interest is to develop the real amateur who wants to build his own machine.

"We hope to put on our own race at Silverstone (Northants) this year, and expect to get nearly 100 of our cars competing."

Cars of Future

Some of the older fraternity of British racing drivers may be inclined to look down their noses, but these tiny speedsters are the cars of the future. More than one ex-Brooklands driver will be racing in them this year.

As an example of the enthusiasm of the young drivers behind this new sport, take a look at nineteen-year-old Stirling Moss, son of Berkshire farmer and former well-known Brooklands driver Alfred Moss.

He only got out of bed this week after a serious illness. But instead of staying quietly at home convalescing this Easter holiday he will be crouching in a tiny cockpit hurtling his silver, bullet-like Cooper "500" round the concrete track at Goodwood, where the road racing season opens on Monday.

Nothing will keep him away. The call of speed is irresistible.

Stirling Moss, one of the "500" competitors at Goodwood on Monday.

BRITISH 'OUTBID' FOR TITLE FIGHT

From RON FRANKS

Durban, Friday.

NEWS that George Dingley, manager of British and Empire feather-weight champion Ronnie Clayton has agreed to the Blackpool lad defending his Empire title here against Tony Lombard on July 1—subject to British Boxing Board approval—has set Durban afire.

Lombard's run of successes in England has captured the imagination of the whole public, and the people are

THE British Grand Prix has seen plenty of high-octane thrills and spills since drivers first got the green light for the event in 1926 at Brooklands.

For UK motorsport enthusiasts, the annual highlight of the calendar has most often taken place at Silverstone since the introduction of the World Drivers' Championship in 1950.

With the circuit likely to stage its final event this year, Great British Grand Prix Heroes is a celebration of some of the men who combined concentration, tactical know-how and supreme skill in quenching their need for speed.

Featuring rare and iconic images from one of the greatest picture archives in the country, this Mirror collection captures the full glory of the British Grand Prix and some of the Brits who have helped make it what it is.

It also delves into the vaults of the Mirror archive to reflect on some of the stories behind the pictures.

Featuring the likes of Hawthorn, Hunt, Hill and Hamilton, Moss and Mansell, Surtees and Stewart, Great British Grand Prix Heroes is a souvenir to savour.

Page 10

DAILY EXPRESS INTERNATIONAL TROPHY MEETING
SILVERSTONE 1951

1st DUNLOP

500 cc Race
1st 2nd & 3rd

Production Car Races
1st in all 6 Classes

(Subject to Official Confirmation)

The World's Master Tyre

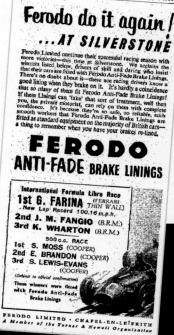

PAGE 10   DAILY MIRROR, Monday, July 20, 1953

Ferodo do it again!
...AT SILVERSTONE

Ferodo Limited continue their successful racing season with more victories—this time at Silverstone. We acclaim the winners listed below, drivers of skill and daring who insist that their cars are fitted with Ferodo Anti-Fade Brake Linings. There's no doubt about it—these ace racing drivers know a good lining when they brake on it. It's hardly a coincidence that so many of them fit Ferodo Anti-Fade Brake Linings! If these Linings can 'take' that sort of treatment, well then you, the private motorist, can rely on them with complete confidence. It's because they're so safe, so reliable, such smooth workers that Ferodo Anti-Fade Brake Linings are fitted as standard equipment on the majority of British cars—a thing to remember when you have your brakes re-lined.

FERODO
ANTI-FADE BRAKE LININGS

International Formula Libre Race
1st G. FARINA (FERRARI THIN WALL)
New Lap Record 100.16 m.p.h.
2nd J. M. FANGIO (B.R.M.)
3rd K. WHARTON (B.R.M.)

500 c.c. RACE
1st S. MOSS (COOPER)
2nd E. BRANDON (COOPER)
3rd S. LEWIS-EVANS (COOPER)

(Subject to official confirmation)

These winners were fitted with Ferodo Anti-Fade Brake Linings

FERODO LIMITED · CHAPEL-EN-LE-FRITH
A Member of the Turner & Newall Organisation

The cutting from the Daily Mirror in 1949 above announces the arrival of the 500cc car, and it wasn't long before it took Silverstone by storm (right)

A pit stop for Giuseppe Farina at the 1951 race, while, on the opposite page, the Daily Mirror features a teenage Stirling Moss

Jose Froilan Gonzalez (24) and eventual winner Alberto Ascari (5) lead the field at the start in 1953

Dust flies at the start in 1965. Jim Clark's
Lotus (5) is just disappearing out of frame.
The Scot eventually won by three seconds
from Graham Hill, his fourth consecutive
British Grand Prix triumph

The start in 1954: Note the relaxed bystanders at the side of the track, an unthinkable sight these days

Man of the day: Clark waves to the crowd at the end of the '65 race

Chaos after a multiple pile-up at the start in 1973. Eleven cars were forced to retire after South African Jody Scheckter lost control of his car coming out of the Woodcote corner at the end of the first lap

Graham Hill leads the pack at the 1969 race, which was won by Jackie Stewart

FACT FILE:

CIRCUIT LENGTH: *3.194 miles*

NUMBER OF LAPS: *60*

LAP RECORD: *1m18.739s (Michael Schumacher, Ferrari, 2004)*

FASTEST CORNER:
Becketts – a top-gear sweeping right-hander

• Half the circuit is in Northamptonshire and half in Buckinghamshire.
• It is built on the site of a Second World War bomber base, RAF Silverstone.
• It hosted the inaugural Formula One World Championship race, on May 13 1950.
• The 2009 British Grand Prix will be the 59th to have counted towards the World Championship. Italy is the only other nation to have appeared on the calendar every season since its inception in 1950.
• The first Grand Prix races at Silverstone were held on the runways themselves.

• Peter Collins was the first Briton to win a British Grand Prix at Silverstone, winning in a Ferrari in 1958.

• Since then, Jim Clark, Jackie Stewart, James Hunt, John Watson, Nigel Mansell, Johnny Herbert, David Coulthard and Lewis Hamilton have all won the event at the circuit.

• In recent years, the British Grand Prix has generated about £65 million annually for Silverstone's local economy.

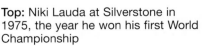

09

Top: Niki Lauda at Silverstone in 1975, the year he won his first World Championship

Middle: David Coulthard takes the chequered flag in 2000, a race controversially staged in April

Bottom: Jacques Villeneuve leads the field into Copse corner at the start in 1996 – the Canadian won the race

68 **M SPORT** | Daily Mirror SATURDAY 21.06.2008

FORMULA ONE BRIT ROW ON EVE OF FRENCH GP

Lewis hails 'class & character' of home GP circuit

SAVE OUR SILVERSTONE

TIME FOR REFLECTION
Hamilton reflected in a fire marshal's helmet at Magny-Cours in France yesterday

10

I WON'T STRIKE, SAYS ACE

From **BYRON YOUNG**

BRITISH hope Lewis Hamilton ruled out taking part in a drivers' strike that could ruin the British Grand Prix.

Leading racers, including Fernando Alonso (below), yesterday insisted they were considering united action over a four-fold increase in the fee for the super-licence that allows them to compete in F1.

After saying he backed the other drivers, Hamilton yesterday ruled out protest action.

He said: "I am not involved in any strike talks, that is not my position.

"I am here to race, to do my job for the team, for myself and for the fans of Formula One.

"I don't believe drivers will take such drastic measures."

▶ **FLYING THE FLAG** Hamilton is keen to help

BY BYRON YOUNG
b.young@mirror.co.uk

LEWIS HAMILTON has issued an emotional plea to help save the British Grand Prix at Silverstone, describing the track as "real class".

F1 ringmaster Bernie Ecclestone revealed yesterday that negotiations with circuit owners the BRDC are deadlocked and he is in advance talks that could change the face of the nation's biggest motorsport event.

If Silverstone does not complete its ambitious building programme on schedule, billionaire Ecclestone has threatened to move the race to Donington in the Midlands or strip Britain of its place on the calendar altogether.

Hamilton takes part in qualifying in France today – the last race before the British Grand Prix in a fortnight, and he spoke out on behalf of the Northamptonshire track which is carrying out a multi-million pound development programme.

"I don't get involved in politics, I refuse to, but anything I can do to help I will," said Hamilton.

"Business is stronger and the event stands a stronger chance of staying now. We can't lose this circuit.

"It has real character, real class and has been around for years.

"If we lose it Formula One wouldn't be the same."

After his historic victory at Monaco last month in the world's greatest motor race, Hamilton admits his home

Grand Prix is the next, and biggest, target on his agenda.

"This is the one," he added. "We all aspire to win Monaco just because of its history and the fact that it's a street circuit means there is nothing like it.

"But winning your home

> **We can't lose this circuit. F1 just wouldn't be the same** – Lewis Hamilton

Grand Prix is an incredible feeling, even different to Monaco because its your home country, has got your home crowd and more British supporters all waving more flags than any country we go to.

"You go into it with a real sense of being proud, a real sense of your family being there. It's definitely the one we work very hard for. This year it's going to be tough for me to win.

"I'm in a much stronger position than last year to win this Grand Prix so I'm quite relaxed about it but it's gong to be tough. Winning my

home race would be very emotional."

After being hit with a 10-place grid penalty for crashing into title rival Kimi Raikkonen in the pitlane in Canada, Hamilton knows his chances of a victory in tomorrow's race here in France are slim.

"I'm always aiming to win but realistically we have to try and aim for the podium," he added.

"We are all very close and it's not easy to overtake so I will keep my fingers crossed and hope we can push it into the top five."

Even though he is unlikely to arrive in front of his sell-out home crowd at Silverstone leading the championship, there is every chance he could be there when he leaves, especially if makes the delirious journey to the top of the podium.

DRIVERS' CHAMPIONSHIP

1	R Kubica (Pol) BMW Sauber	42 pts
2	L Hamilton (GB) McLaren	38
3	F Massa (Bra) Ferrari	38
4	K Raikkonen (Fin) Ferrari	35
5	N Heidfeld (Ger) BMW Sauber	28
6	H Kovalainen (Fin) McLaren	15
7	M Webber (Aus) Red Bull	15
8	J Trulli (Ita) Toyota	12
9	F Alonso (Spa) Renault	9
10	N Rosberg (Ger) Williams	8
11	K Nakajima (Jpn) Williams	7
12	D Coulthard (GB) Red Bull	6
13	T Glock (Ger) Toyota	5
14	S Vettel (Ger) Toro Rosso	5
15	R Barrichello (Bra) Honda	5
16	J Button (GB) Honda	3

TOSELAND REVEALS NAKED AMBITION

▲ **READY TO RAW** Toseland's Donington dare

JAMES TOSELAND has promised his army of fans he will do his victory lap NAKED if he wins tomorrow's British MotoGP at Donington Park.

The 27-year-old celebrated a double World Superbike victory at Brands Hatch last August by throwing his leathers into the crowd. His modesty was saved by a pair of lycra shorts – but the Tech3 Yamaha rider has vowed it is all coming off if he becomes the first Brit in 27 years to win a top-class race.

"If I win at Donington this weekend not only the leathers will be coming off but the pants as well," said Toseland,

who is seventh in the title race after seven races. "If I can get up there on the podium I don't mind – as long as I've got my bike to cover me up then I'm fine.

"I've done it before when I did a shoot for Cosmopolitan magazine naked. But it's the sort of thing you might look

back on and find quite embarrassing." And Toseland says he aims to end 27 years of British failure and insists he will handle the pressure.

"It has been far too long since we last had success," added Toseland, who had just been born when Barry Sheene won his last race.

▲ **STRIP TEASE** Toseland vows to reveal all

Celebrities at Silverstone, clockwise from top left:
David and Victoria Beckham get police protection in 2007; Sir Jackie Stewart with Olympic rowing gold medallist James Cracknell and tennis player Tim Henman in 2001; Damon Hill greets Tony Blair and wife Cherie before the 1996 race; a kiss for Jenson Button from Chris Evans in 2000; Simon Le Bon, Sir Stirling Moss, Natasha Bedingfield, Frankie Dettori, a guest and Yasmin Le Bon in 2007; George Harrison, who was a huge motor racing fan, at Silverstone in 1977; Sylvester Stallone behind the camera in 1998; a young Prince William in the cockpit of a Benetton

MIKE HAWTHORN

Daily Mirror
MON OCT 20 1958

2½ FORWARD WITH THE PEOPLE   No. 17,060

RACE OF THE CENTURY DRAMA

Moss wins—MIKE is the CHAMPION

From PETER STEPHENS, Casablanca, Sunday

BRITISH racing ace Stirling Moss won the "race of the century" at Casablanca, Morocco, today with a breathtaking victory over his British rival Mike Hawthorn.

But Hawthorn took second place—and that was enough for **HIM** to win the World Racing Drivers' Championship.

This was the last Grand Prix of the season—and Hawthorn's final aggregate of forty-two points was **one** better than Moss's total.

Moss had hoped to w i p e o u t Hawthorn's points lead with this one race and win the title.

As admirers c r o w d e d round them after the race Moss shook hands with Hawthorn and said wryly: "You got it after all, you old so-and-so."

The race was marred by two accidents. Fair-haired Stuart Lewis-Evans, of Britain, driving a Vanwall, skidded on a patch of oil and spun off the track.

He crawled out of the blazing car and ran along the track, his clothes in flames.

Last night doctors at the hospital where Lewis-Evans

Always Led

Hurling his dark-green British Vanwall around the track Moss led from start to finish in the 249-mile race.

But Hawthorn was always there, trailing him in his flame-red Italian Ferrari.

Moss's average speed was

was taken said that his condition was grave.

They said burns covered three-quarters of his body.

In the other accident French driver Francois Picard and Oliver Gendebien of Belgium were injured when their cars crashed. Picard was said to have several broken bones.

—AND BRITON CRASHES

116.4 miles per hour—and he set up a lap record with a blistering 119.3 m.p.h.

Moss's time for the race was 2h. 9m. 15s. Hawthorn's time was 2h. 10m. 39.8s.

Phil Hill, of America, was third in a Ferrari.

Later Hawthorn celebrated his championship in CHAMPAGNE with his pit crew.

Moss, a teetotaller, drank to his race victory with—a FRUIT JUICE.

Juan Fangio, of Argentina, who was the previous holder of the championship —he has retired from racing—said tonight:

"British drivers have come back into the racing limelight in a really big way."

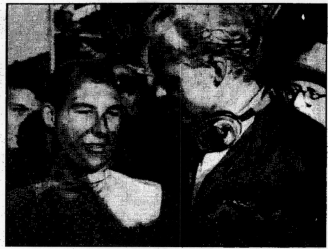

● Stirling Moss (left), who won the race, congratulates Mike Hawthorn, who was second—but who scored enough points to give him the world racing drivers' championship.

Shirley Sanders and Robert Kardell pictured after their Hollywood wedding

A 'BRAIN' PICKED THE BRIDE

AMERICA has found the "gimmick to beat all gimmicks"—an electronic brain that CHOOSES BRIDES.

Each week personal details of applicants are fed into, and sorted by, the "cupid with coils" on the coast-to-coast television show "People are funny." The machine chooses couples who seem to be best suited to each other.

But only one couple out of thirty-five have so far taken the machine's advice. Shirley Sanders and Robert Kardell, both twenty-six.

They are pictured here after their wedding yesterday.

Following them are the bride's sister Karen and television star Art Linkletter, who introduced them to the "brain."

Shirley and Bob won £7,000 on the show and a "bonus" honeymoon in Honolulu.

12

FACTFILE:
Born: Mexborough, 10.04.29.
Died: 22.01.59.
Teams: LD Hawthorn, AHM Bryde, Ferrari, Vanwall, BRM.
F1 wins: 3.

Podium positions: 18.
World championships: 1 (1958).
Pole positions: 4.
British GP wins: 0.
First win: 1953 French GP.
Last win: 1958 French GP.

From the top:
Mike Hawthorn climbs into his Ferrari prior to the 1953 British Grand Prix; below, he is seen going though Copse corner on the way to finishing fifth. The black and white image shows Hawthorn following Stirling Moss and Archie Scott-Brown at the 1956 race.
Bottom: he inspects his Ferrari with friend and team-mate Peter Collins

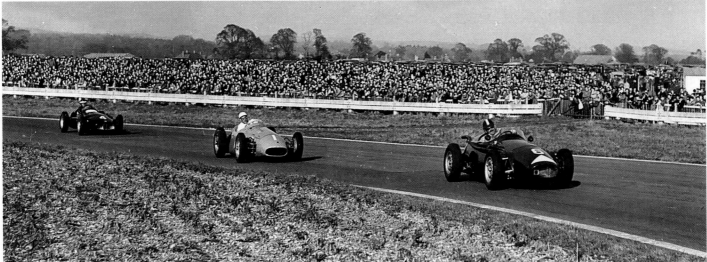

After finishing an impressive fourth in his debut Grand Prix in Belgium in 1952, Hawthorn was signed up by Ferrari in 1953. Sporting his trademark spotted bow tie, the Yorkshire-born driver won his first Grand Prix that July, at Reims.

Hawthorn patriotically left Ferrari for the new Vanwall team in 1955, although he contemplated quitting racing altogether after being blamed by a section of the press for the horrific accident which killed more than 80 spectators (the exact number has never been recorded) at Le Mans that year. Hawthorn went on to win the 24-hour race.

After an unsuccessful season at BRM, he rejoined Ferrari in 1957 and the following year won the world championship, pipping Stirling Moss by one point after finishing second in the final race of the season at Casablanca.

On becoming champion, Hawthorn promptly announced his retirement. He had clearly been shaken by the death of his close friend Peter Collins at the Nürburgring a few months earlier. Tragically, Hawthorn died in January 1959 in a car accident on his way to a function to celebrate his championship success.

PETER COLLINS

RACING ACE COLLINS SACRIFICES HIS TITLE

FANGIO

COLLINS—Toast of the town

By PATRICK MENNEM

WITH a dramatic gesture of good sportsmanship British motor racing ace Peter Collins, from Kidderminster, yesterday cheerfully gave up his chance of winning the title of World Champion Driver.

All he had to do to earn that title was to keep his position of third in the field of the 300-mile Grand Prix of Europe at Monza, Italy.

His only rival for the world championship title—awarded for points gained in races throughout the year—had been forced out of the race by wheel failure.

The rival was Collins's Ferrari team-mate, Juan Fangio of Argentina, present holder of the world title, which he has won three times.

First Ever

Fangio, 45, hoped to be the first man ever to win the championship four times—and now, it seemed, the chance had gone.

He was sitting glumly in the pits when suddenly Collins's car roared in for tyre changing.

Collins jumped out and said:

"Here, take over Juan."

Fangio kissed Collins on the cheek, jumped into the Ferrari and roared away to a burst of cheering from the huge crowd.

Second

From that moment Collins was out of the running for the World Championship, for this was the last race counting in the points table.

Fangio went on to finish second to Britain's Stirling Moss.

So Fangio DID make history by becoming cham-

Let Fangio drive car

pion for the fourth time with 30 points.

Stirling Moss, who drove his Maserati at an average speed of 129.6 m.p.h., finished second in the world rating with 27 points.

Peter Collins was only third on the list with 25 points.

Last night Peter, who is twenty-four, said:

"I could not win the race. I was practically convinced that was impossible.

"Fangio, on the other hand, needed only one point to win the world championship. So I gave him the car."

Astonished

"The important thing, after all, was that one man on my team could clinch the title."

Fangio said: "I was astonished when he handed over his car. But I did not stop to argue.

"In fact Peter pushed me into the car. He still had a great chance to win his world title when he handed it over. I know how much that renunciation meant to him.

"This is one of the things that make a friendship really great."

Fangio added: "I do not know whether, in Collins's place, I would have done the same."

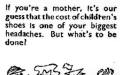

1946 MURDER POLICE TO OPEN GRAVE

THE body of a woman, murdered ten years ago is to be exhumed early tomorrow morning. The woman, Mrs. Olive Michelle Nixon, a fifty-seven-year-old widow, was found battered to death near Regent's Park in November, 1946. Her grave is at Midhurst, Sussex.

The decision to exhume the woman was taken at a conference at Scotland Yard.

When the body is exhumed, Dr. Keith Simpson, the pathologist, watched by Detective - Superintendent John Jamieson, will carry out a post - mortem examination at the graveside.

The exhumation is necessary because Sir Bernard Spilsbury, the famous pathologist who conducted the post-mortem examination on Mrs. Nixon in 1946, is now dead.

Two weeks ago Adam Ogilvie, 32, a labourer, of no fixed address, was charged with the murder of Mrs. Nixon. He is at present in custody.

Weather hits Channel trips

WITH only fifteen days before no-passport trips end, a steamer company running day excursions from Thames estuary resorts announced yesterday that 15,000 fewer passengers went to France this year than last. More than 65,000 went last year.

The manager of the company said: "It's the weather. We have many bookings—for next year."

14

Collins at the 1958 British Grand Prix at Silverstone, his final race win. He was killed just two weeks later

A TRAGIC accident in the German Grand Prix of 1958 robbed motorsport of one of its great gentlemen.

He began his career in tiny 500cc rear-engined racing cars before progressing to the HWM team with whom he made his F1 debut in the Swiss Grand Prix of 1952.

He was chosen to debut the Vanwall thin-wall special in its first Grand Prix in 1954 before switching to Maserati. This brought him to the attention of Enzo Ferrari who hired him for 1956. Collins got his first Grand Prix win in the Lancia-Ferrari in Belgium and his second in France a month later.

In a typical act of sportsmanship later that season, he agreed to hand his car over to team-mate Juan Manuel Fangio at Monza, allowing the Argentine to clinch the championship and ending Collins' own hopes.

He won his final Grand Prix in 1958, fittingly at Silverstone, before his life was cut short at the age of 26 just two weeks later. Battling it out with the Vanwall of Tony Brooks in Germany, Collins ran wide, his Ferrari flying up a bank and flinging him clear. He died later that day of severe head injuries.

FACTFILE:
Born: Kidderminster, 06.11.31.
Died: 03.08.58.
Teams: HWM, Vanwall, Maserati, Ferrari.
F1 wins: 3.
Podium positions: 9.
World championships: 0.
Pole positions: 0.
British GP wins: 1 (1958).
First win: 1956 Belgian GP.
Last win: 1958 British GP.

SIR STIRLING MOSS

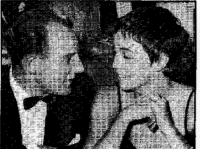

Vicky
WITH APOLOGIES TO H.M.V.

Too long-playing record

Stirling and his wife, Katie.

SKYLARKING STIRLING WINS—WITH A BAD EYE

STIRLING MOSS, British motor racing ace, roared to victory in the Argentine Grand Prix yesterday IN SPITE OF an eye injury.

His wife, Katie, 22, accidentally stuck a finger in his left eye while they were "skylarking," at the week-end.

And Stirling, 28, had to go to hospital. He said after treatment: "My vision is blurred."

A doctor examined him half an hour before the race at Buenos Aires yesterday and said he could drive. But Stirling said that his vision was still blurred.

But just before the "off," he removed a bandage from his injured eye and said that he WOULD drive.

Driving a Cooper-Climax, Moss crept up to third place by the start of the second lap.

Mobbed

Moss seized the lead when Fangio (Maserati) —five times world motor-racing champion—pulled into the pits to change a wheel in the thirty-fifth lap.

He was mobbed as he roared in at the end of the eighty-lap race. Katie rewarded him with a kiss.

Mike Hawthorn (Ferrari) was third, and Fangio, who had won the race for the past four years, was fourth.

DOUGLAS JUST BUBBLED OVER

● Bubbles — hundreds of snowy white soapy bubbles—suddenly appeared all over centre half Douglas Chaffin's shorts and socks as he played football in the rain at Probus, Cornwall.

● Then at half-time his wife Sylvia confessed : "It's my fault. I was interrupted by a knock at the door when I was washing Douglas's football kit and I forgot to rinse out the detergent."

STRYDOM: 'BAD HEART'

South African Premier Dr. Strydom, who has been ill for several weeks, is suffering from heart trouble, a medical bulletin issued in Johannesburg said yesterday. Some reports say he will resign soon.

ARMS SEIZED

French halt Red ship

WORLD NEWS SPOTLIGHT

SIX HUNDRED cases of arms were taken yesterday from the hold of a Yugoslav cargo ship which was intercepted off the coast of Algeria—a French North African possession—by two French destroyers.

The destroyers stopped the ship, the 5,800-ton Slovenija, in Algerian territorial waters and ordered it into the Algerian port of Oran.

Armed French troops and police cordoned off the port area while the arms were unloaded and confiscated. Later, the Slovenija put to sea again.

Diplomats say the French authorities feared the arms might have reached anti-French rebels in Algeria.

IN BELGRADE, Yugoslav officials said the Slovenija was bound for Morocco, which borders Algeria.

MACMILLAN SEES SERVICE CHIEFS

☆ Mr. Harold Macmillan, on his Commonwealth tour, yesterday met British Service chiefs in Singapore, reports Associated Press (American).

☆ Main question was believed to be the possibility of using more Australian and New Zealand forces to replace some of the British troops in Malaya. Later Mr. Macmillan left by air for New Zealand.

PLOUGHLAND HUNT FOR ANNE

RECENTLY-PLOUGHED land in the Wheathampstead area of Hertfordshire was searched yesterday in the hunt for Anne Noblett, 17, who vanished on December 30 on her way home from a dancing class.

Essex detectives investigating the murder of Mary Kriek, nineteen-year-old Dutch girl, whose body was found in a ditch at Boxted a fortnight ago, met Dr. Francis Camps, the pathologist, to discuss aspects of the post-mortem examination report.

Daily Mirror

TUES OCT 8 1957

FORWARD WITH THE PEOPLE

2½°

No. 16,740

MOSS WINS AGAIN!

Speed ace Stirling weds his Katie

Speed-ace Stirling Moss wins again—not a car race this time, but a lovely bride. And there, in the picture on the right, is his race track rival Mike Hawthorn, cheering him on with rose-petal confetti.

Yes Stirling wins. Just look at that heart-shaped picture at the top, as he kisses his bride, Katie Molson, after their wedding at St. Peter's, Westminster, yesterday.

Left: Mike Hawthorn, the man who would pip Stirling Moss to the world championship a year later, joins the celebrations at Stirling's 1957 wedding
Below: Moss leads Juan Manuel Fangio at the 1955 British Grand Prix at Aintree. Inches separated the Mercedes team-mates when the chequered flag fell, with Moss the victor

Daily Mirror

TUES FEB 25 1950

2½ FORWARD WITH THE PEOPLE ✦ ✦ ✦ No. 16,858

Rebels spread oil on track, then—

30 KILLED IN BIG RACE CRASH

MORE than thirty people were reported killed last night after a car competing in the Grand Prix at Havana, Cuba skidded on oil spread by rebels, according to agency reports.

The car—a Ferrari, driven by Alberto Carreras, of Cuba—crashed into a crowded stand.

Officials were reported to have declared the race "cancelled because of rebel sabotage."

Fangio

The rebels blamed for the disaster were believed to belong to the "July 26" group, which kidnapped world champion driver Juan Fangio on Sunday night. Their leader is Colonel Fidel Castro.

The start of the race had been delayed ninety minutes in the hope that the forty-six-year-old Argentinian would be released in time to compete.

But when the twenty-seven cars roared off at the starter's signal, Fangio was still missing.

British racing ace Stirling Moss, in a Ferrari, was leading at the time of the crash.

Locked

in Room

Earlier Moss, 28, was put under strong guard after reports that the rebels who kidnapped Fangio were planning to seize him too.

The threat was made a few hours before the start of the race.

Stirling and his attractive wife, Katie, 22, immediately locked themselves in their room.

Hotel detectives were posted outside the door.

Then, when the time came for Moss to go to the racing pits, a

Fangio still held— guard on Moss

heavily-armed police escort arrived to take him and Katie there.

The number of plain-clothes detectives in the pits outnumbered the mechanics working on Moss's car.

More than 1,500 troops and police with guns patrolled the circuit.

'Found' Report

Was False

With minutes to go before the start, a cheer went up from the 30,000 crowd when it was announced by loudspeaker that Fangio had been found.

But the report was FALSE.

As the cars roared round the circuit thousands of troops and police searched Havana, still looking for Fangio.

Then came the crash, and the decision to abandon the race.

The man behind the sabotage—Colonel Fidel Castro (right) pictured gun in hand at a rally of his "July 26" rebels.

BROOKE HOWLED DOWN

DEMONSTRATORS surged towards a platform from which Housing Minister Henry Brooke was defending the Rent Act last night.

Mr. Brooke watched them for a moment, then left the platform for a room at the back.

Shortly afterwards he left the Holborn Hall, London, with a bodyguard of more than a dozen uniformed policemen.

Meantime, the meeting, which had been punctuated with cries of "Resign," "Repeal the Rent Act" and "M-O-S-L-E-Y," had broken up in disorder.

The platform table was upset and chairs were broken. The microphone crashed on one man's head.

Earlier, when the Minister went into the hall, he was showered with "Brooke Must Resign" pamphlets.

Above him were balloons trailing streamer slogans which read: "No Evictions" and "Evict Henry."

When he started to speak he was greeted by boos. As the chairman, Mr. Geoffrey Johnson-Smith, tried to quieten the crowd a man walked towards the platform throwing more leaflets.

These were headed: "Mosley or slump."

Later, Mr. Brooke said: "This was not typical of the people of London."

When he was asked if Fascists had been operating in a body, he said the only people he recognised were Communists.

A great ambassador for British motorsport, Sir Stirling came agonisngly close to the world championship but had to be content with finishing as runner-up on four consecutive occasions in the 1950s.

An adrenaline junkie, his father bought him an old Austin Seven when he was just nine and the young Moss would drive it around the fields surrounding their home. He began racing by putting money he had won as a showjumper towards a sports car. After progressing to a Cooper single seater, he joined the HWM F2 team in 1950. In 1954, Moss bought a Maserati, taking on and beating the legendary Mercedes driver Juan Manuel Fangio to secure a place on the German team.

Aintree was the scene of his first Grand Prix triumph in 1955 but he finished

runner-up in the Drivers' Championship to team-mate Fangio. It would become a familiar feeling. Twelve months later, the same thing happened with Fangio in a Ferrari and Moss back in a Maserati. In 1957, he achieved his dream of winning the British Grand Prix in a British car at Aintree but again lost the title to Fangio before being pipped by compatriot Mike Hawthorn in 1958.

On Easter Monday 1962, Moss was battling Graham Hill at a non-Championship event at Goodwood when his Lotus speared head-on into an earth bank. It took 40 minutes to cut him from the wreckage and 14 months to recover. He attempted a return to racing but felt he no longer had the same command of the car and retired from F1.

FACTFILE:
Born: London, 17.09.29.
Teams: Mercedes-Benz, Maserati, Vanwall, Rob Walker, Cooper, Lotus.
F1 wins: 16. Podium positions: 24.
World championships: 0.
Pole positions: 16.
British GP wins: 2 (1955, 1957).
First win: 1955 British Grand Prix.
Last win: 1961 German Grand Prix.

Above: Showing precise control at the wet 1961 British Grand Prix at Aintree. Sporting a Beatles wig in 1963 (right)

GRAHAM HILL

On the circuit where a sport was born..

Graham Hill, showing his children the magic of Brooklands

WAR IN SCHOOLS

—and urges their to report any signs :-taking immediately. William says that where there is no the school doctor be consulted imme- when a boy or girl spected of taking

on how to spot -taking among ters are given by i's school medical er. Dr. Alexander i.

Danger signs to watch for include:
SUSPICIOUS changes in the behaviour pattern of pupils. Absences on Mondays may be a pointer, since many young people use drugs only, or mainly, at the weekend.
WILD ELATION, talkativeness or depression without reasonable cause, and extra tiredness or sleepiness after the weekend.
LOSS of interest and unwillingness to conform to

normally co-operative pupils.
London is now at least the fourth education authority to ask its teachers to join the war against drug-taking by youngsters.
A spokesman for the Inner London Education Authority said: "There is no evidence as such that there is drug-taking in London's schools." This is merely a precautionary measure."

THEY look like a family enjoying a simple afternoon in the country. But for racing driver Graham Hill, his wife and children, it is the setting that is special.

For this is Brooklands. A name still spoken in a hushed, reverent tone by those who know about motor racing. And who remember this as the very birthplace of the sport.

Now, as you can see, the trees push their way through the concrete banking. There's a car park where the pits were. And a British Aircraft

NOW . . ONLY MEMORIES

Corporation factory where the crowds used to roar.

It's getting on for thirty years since the last driver took the last chequered flag. But this tiny corner of Surrey evokes a flood of memories.

Memories of gentlemen in lounge suits racing quaint cars around the two-and-three-quarter-mile circuit. Of the first daring woman to break into this man's world. Of famous

names like Malcolm Campbell . . . and the great John Cobb who once lapped there at 143 m.p.h.

An age sadly dead. But Brooklands still has a powerful magic that draws the race aces of today. Like former world champion Graham Hill, pictured with his wife Bette and their children Bridget, Damon and baby Samantha.

To them, and all the racing fraternity, this—in spite of the weeds—is hallowed ground. And always will be.

Picture by Mirror Cameraman
FREDDIE REED

FACTFILE:
Born: Hampstead,
15.02.29.
Died: 29.11.75.
Teams: Lotus, BRM,
Brabham, Hill.
F1 wins: 14. Podium
positions: 36.

World championships: 2
(1962, 1968).
Pole positions: 13.
British GP wins: 0.
First win: 1962 Dutch Grand
Prix.
Last win: 1969 Monaco
Grand Prix.

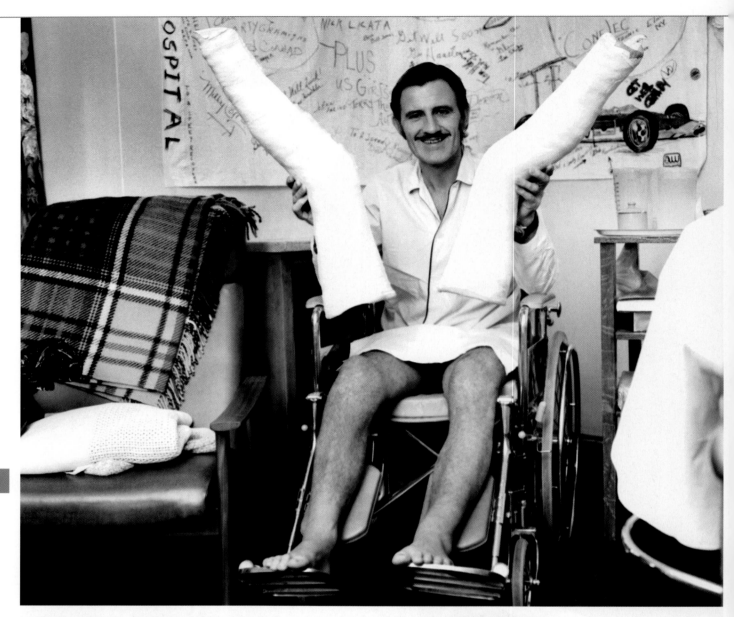

Above: An accident in 1969 had left Hill lying in plaster at the University College Hospital, London. He looks cheerful as the casts are removed. Behind him is a huge get well card

Left: Sitting deep in thought at Brands Hatch after learning of the death of Jo Siffert in 1971

Opposite top: In his BRM during the British Grand Prix at Silverstone in July 1965

Opposite bottom: At Snetterton in 1964

Daily Mirror

4d. Tuesday, May 31, 1966 ✦ No. 19,419

11 46

Triumph after 16-car pile-up in big race

HILL WINS FOR BRITAIN AT INDIANAPOLIS

The Tote pays out on the LAST horse

THE Tote paid out on the LAST horse in a race yesterday. There were angry protests by punters.

It happened at a National Hunt meeting at Fakenham, Norfolk. Book End, a 6-1 outsider, ridden by George Appleby, was well behind in last place.

Mistake

But to everyone's amazement Book End was placed SECOND by the judge, Lord Somerleyton. And Guinness was listed among the also-rans.

Much later, when all the winnings had been paid, the Fakenham officials discovered their mistake.

And Mr. V. J. Lucas, the clerk of the course, said that No. 1, Guinness, should have been placed second and NOT No. 13, Book End.

But by that time the bookies had gone home.

Lord Somerleyton said later: "There was a certain similarity of colours, and I placed the wrong one second."

A winning debut

Graham Hill. . . . He won the race brilliantly at his first attempt.

ENGLAND'S Graham Hill won the Indianapolis "500" today, the world's greatest motor race.

World champion Jim Clark, the flying Scot who won the race last year, drove brilliantly to snatch second place.

Twice he fought his way out of terrifying skids—then his car developed suspension trouble.

Another Scot, Jackie Stewart, was leading with only eight laps to go—then his car spluttered to a halt.

It was Hill's first attempt at the race. His 36-year-old wife Betty watched the race being televised "live" in a

---

From JOHN SMITH
Indianapolis, Monday.

London cinema via the Early Bird satellite.

As Hill flashed past the line she whooped with joy.

"It's absolutely marvellous," she said.

"It's the first time he has ever been to Indianapolis. I'm thrilled more than I can say."

The race began with a fantastic pile-up. Sixteen cars crashed in a blazing heap of wreckage only seconds after the start.

Miraculously, only one driver was injured—not seriously.

The cars crashed at 120 miles an hour as they raced for the first bend.

Wheels were ripped off and hurtled through the air as machines slammed into each other.

Two cars burst into flames and a 7ft. wall of fire seared across the track.

Stewart and Hill, both driving Ford Lolas, were trapped momentarily in the crash area, about 800 yards from the starting grid

Three cars crashed immediately behind Hill So did two in front of him.

Swerve

But both he and Stewart were able to swerve clear of the chaos.

One car disintegrated as it hit the banking. Two wheels hurtled through the air amid a shower of sparks.

Cars tightly bunched behind crunched into the crippled car.

More wheels were torn off.

The only casualty among the drivers was Texan A. J. Foyt, a previous winner of the race.

His injuries: A cut finger and a bruised left knee.

About twelve spectators were treated for shock and minor cuts.

The race was halted for only the second time in its fifty-year history. The previous occasion was in 1964, when two drivers died in a seven-car smash.

Clark, in a Ford Lotus, missed the pile-up and roared into the lead on the seventeenth of the 200 laps.

Then on the 65th lap he spun on to grass alongside the track, righted himself, drove into the pits and refuelled.

Cool

Clark again went into a spin on lap 85.

But in a display of cool mastery, he straightened the car after three turns and made a lightning 21-second pit stop.

Hill, world driving champion in 1962, said after the race: "I was rather surprised to win, but I'm very pleased. The car ran beautifully."

Of the thirty-three starters only six finished.

Hill's speed for the race was 144.317 mph. Clark's winning speed last year was a record 150.686.

HOW IT STARTED

Start of the big pile-up. Two tyres spiral into the air as a car slams into the bank. Soon, the track was littered with wreckage.

24

ARTHUR SIDEY CLICKED ON AS GRAHAM HILL HURTLED OVER 100 mph. HILL CRASHED, SURVIVED. OUR LUCKY DAY, BOTH SAID

I remember saying to myself as Graham's car got nearer: Is this your last picture, Arthur?

DAILY MIRROR, Tuesday, December 22, 1964   PAGE 17

GRAHAM Hill is the only driver to win the Triple Crown of F1 World Championship, Le Mans and Indianapolis 500; little wonder his career proved such an inspiration to his son Damon.

He bought his first car, a Morris 8, as a 24th birthday present and drove it across London – the first time he had been behind the wheel. He later went to work for Lotus where owner Colin Chapman gave him the requisite parts to build himself a Lotus XI racer on condition that Chapman retained ownership and received all prize monies!

Hill signed for the team in 1957 and when Lotus decided to enter F1 racing the following year, Hill suddenly found himself cast in the role of Grand Prix driver. It wasn't until 1962, in a BRM, that he won his first Grand Prix, at the same Goodwood weekend that effectively ended Sir Stirling Moss's career. By the final race of that season Hill and Jim Clark both had half-a-dozen victories apiece but Clark's breakdown in South Africa handed Hill the title.

Hill rejoined Lotus in 1967 and won a second World Championship in 1968.

He retired from racing in 1975, running his own Embassy Hill team, but he and his five team-mates were tragically killed in November of that year when Hill's light aircraft crashed in fog near Elstree Airport.

Above, main image:
Arthur Sidey's spectacular photograph taken as Graham Hill left a wet track during the Daily Mirror international trophy race at Snetterton in 1964 and headed towards the lens

Hill calmly walks away after surveying the scene following his accident at Snetterton in March 1964. It was the race debut for the BRM P261

A six-year-old Damon Hill in Lotus race overalls as dad Graham checks lap times during qualifying

Family man: Graham pictured spending time with his eldest children Brigitte and Damon. The second picture below also shows youngest daughter Samantha being carried by wife Betty

Mirror

The Daily Mirror Newspapers, Ltd., 1964

Telephone:
FLEet-street 0246

Clark drops out in car race drama

SURTEES—THE NEW WORLD CHAMP

Before yesterday's Mexican Grand Prix race . . . the man who won, Dan Gurney of California (left) talks with the man who took the world motor racing championship, John Surtees, of Britain.

From HOWARD JOHNSON, Mexico City, Sunday

JOHN SURTEES of Britain is the new world motor racing champion. In a sensational finish to the Mexican Grand Prix here today, Jim Clark was robbed of retaining the championship in the very last lap.

After leading all the way for 64 gruelling laps over 200 miles of circuit, Clark's Lotus developed engine trouble and he had to retire.

Dan Gurney, of America, driving a Brabham, came first, Surtees, in a Ferrari, came second, and Italy's Lorenzo Bandini, also in a Ferrari, third.

So Surtees, former world motor-cycling champion, gained six points, bringing him to 40 and one point in the championship tables ahead of Graham Hill.

Hill lagged after the 30th lap when his B R M bumped with Bandini's Ferrari and bent his exhaust pipes.

Vital

Bandini was lying second after Clark had to retire. Surtees passed him in the last stages and so collected his vital points.

An 80,000 crowd, including the Duke of Edinburgh and the President of Mexico, watched the race, the tenth and last to count for the world championship.

A great shout of sympathy went up as Clark's car retired.

The Duke of Edinburgh, who is on a nine-day visit to Mexico, made a point of going to sympathise with Clark after congratulating Surtees.

He told Clark, No. 1 driver in the Lotus team: "You need a lot of luck in this business."

Cost

Said Clark: "It was just bad luck—the worst possible." And later, Clark commented with a shrug: "It's all in the jackpot.

"I think it was a moral victory for me. But moral victories don't win championships."

The trouble w h i c h robbed Clark of the championship also cost him at least £40,000—the money he could have expected to earn as champion in the coming year.

Surtees said of becoming world champion: "It was fantastic. I never thought I had a chance."

TV variety men win big pay rise

VARIETY artists have just won a big pay rise after a three-year battle with B B C Television.

New agreed-minimum fees announced yesterday by Mr. Reg Swinson, secretary of the Variety Artists' Federation are 30 guineas for established performers and 20 guineas for those not so well known.

Wilson points the way

Continued from Page One

an all-out drive on overseas markets;

BOOST import - saving industries, making sure that as far as possible, the sort of product which can be made at home IS made at home instead of being imported; and

IMPROVE facilities available to the small exporter. One of the ways in which this could be done is on a group basis.

It is also likely that the Government will announce that it is going to exercise its borrowing rights under the International Monetary Fund—where we have a stand - by c r e d i t of £357,000,000.

This would see Britain through her immediate difficulties.

Theme

There will be no return to the stop - go - stop economy of the Tories. The main theme of the Labour plan will be the long as well as short term aims.

expansion linked with the cutting out of waste.

Under this heading, Ministers may disclose that they are taking a hard look at some of the projects launched by the Tories for prestige reasons.

These include the Channel Tunnel scheme, the Concord—a supersonic airliner planned to be built as a joint effort with France — and the proposed new Cunard liner "Q4."

Reaction

Today's economic statement will cover long as well as short term aims.

Tory reaction to the Government's plan will be provided b y the ex-Chancellor, Mr. Maudling, at a special Press conference.

Tonight the Tories will keep a sharp eye on the Premier's broadcast.

If, in their view, he makes a party political speech, they will be quick to demand s i m i l a r T V time for a Tory spokesman.

What the Mirror Says— See Page Two.

FIVE KILLED IN CRASH

FIVE people were killed in a three-car pile-up early today. Three other people were seriously injured in the crash—on an "S" bend two miles from Exeter on the Plymouth road. Firemen used flame cutters to free the injured from the wreckage.

COLOUR ROW ON A BUS TRIP

FIFTY officials, including Cabinet Ministers, staged a protest at the border of white-ruled Rhodesia yesterday.

The officials had been guests at the independence celebrations of Zambia, formerly Northern Rhodesia.

They were on a bus trip to Victoria Falls, on the Zambesi river border between Zambia and Rhodesia.

But when the bus reached the Rhodesian border post, guards ordered them to leave the bus and show their passports.

They were then told to separate—"Coloureds over there, whites over here."

The party protested—and the Israeli Foreign Minister, Mrs. Golda Meir, is understood to have fainted.

Later, the whole group refused to cross the border.

30

John Surtees at the Isle of
Man TT races in March 1957

31

33

Top left: Surtees gets a push from the Ferrari
mechanics at Silverstone in July 1963
Bottom left and this page: In his Ferrari
number one car at the British Grand Prix at
Silverstone in 1965

FACTFILE:
Born: Tatsfield, 11.02.34.
Teams: Lotus, Cooper, Lola,
Ferrari, Honda, BRM,
McLaren, Surtees.
F1 wins: 6.
Podium positions: 24.
World championships: 1
(1964).
Pole positions: 8.
British GP wins: 0.
First win: 1963 German
Grand Prix.
Last win: 1967 Italian GP.

THE greatest racer of all time? Surtees is the only man to have won the World Drivers' Championship on two wheels and four.

The Surrey-born champion won the 350cc motorcycle world title in 1958, 1959 and 1960, and the 500cc title in 1956, 1958, 1959 and 1960. In 1959, he won every single race in both 350cc and 500cc categories.

That same year, he started considering a switch from motorbikes to motorcars and did enough to convince Lotus owner Colin Chapman to hand him an opportunity in 1960. In his second Grand Prix, he finished runner-up to Jack Brabham but it would be 1963 before he clinched his first win – for Ferrari in Germany.

In 1964, he achieved the incredible double of following his motorbike successes by winning the F1 World Drivers' Championship, dramatically securing the title on the final lap of the final race in Mexico, edging out Graham Hill by a single point.

JIM CLARK

VICTORY TOAST—BY GRAND PRIX JIM

By PATRICK MENNEM, Mirror Motoring Reporter

DARK-HAIRED Jim Clark, the Scots lad with the winning ways, raced into second place in the world championship by winning the Daily Mirror-sponsored British Grand Prix at Aintree on Saturday.

He is just one point behind Graham Hill, who has 19 points.

Jim and his Lotus 25 led from start to finish in Saturday's race. But the win was not as easy as it looked.

CHAMPAGNE for Jim Clark . . . from the Daily Mirror Cup.

Seconds

After the race, which was organised by the British Automobile Racing Club, Jim told me:

"I had a great deal of trouble trying to shake off John Surtees.

Over and out .. unhurt

"It was not until halfway through the race that I began to make any impression on him."

John squeezed into second place at the end of the second lap, and for many laps he was only ten seconds behind Jim.

Then John's Lola car went "off song."

Although he held second place, he was almost a

WORLD TITLE NEARER

minute behind Jim at the end of the 75-lap race.

The British Grand Prix emphasised that the combination of Jim Clark and the new Lotus 25 is almost unbeatable.

Graham Hill finished fourth in his B.R.M. and managed to snatch three points in the championship race to keep him in the lead.

He was handicapped on the Aintree circuit by having a five-speed gearbox. The other cars had six gears.

None of the Continental cars earned any points or glory.

Faded

Phil Hill, reigning world champion, retired with mechanical trouble in his Ferrari in the forty-seventh lap. Dan Gurney, the No. 1 Porsche driver, held third place for a few laps, but gradually drifted out of the race.

Third place went to Bruce McLaren in a Cooper. Jack Brabham in a Lotus was fifth.

Jim Clark's average speed was 92.25 m.p.h. And he clocked the fastest lap at 93.91 m.p.h.

● Leaders in the world championship after Graham Hill and Jim Clark are Bruce McLaren with 16 pts. and Phil Hill with 14 pts.

Art raid clue in the park

By MIRROR REPORTER

GARDENER Charlie Coleman, picking up litter in Hyde Park, has given detectives their first clues to the £400,000 Mayfair art theft.

Charlie, 54, found the frames of twelve of the thirty - five paintings stolen in the raid on the O'Hana art gallery in Carlos-place twelve days ago.

The frames—in two sacks—were leaning against a tree in the park. The spot is only half a mile from the gallery.

Charlie took the frames to the police, and experts checked them for fingerprints.

Why ?

The other twenty-three stolen paintings were cut from their frames in the gallery.

Last night Detective Superintendent Ronald Townsend, who is in charge of the inquiries, was trying to discover why the thieves left the frames in the park.

The thirty-five stolen pictures were insured for about £250,000.

A £20,000 reward has been offered for the recovery of the paintings.

BERLIN WALL BLAST

An explosion ripped a hole 8ft. by 3ft. in the Communist wall dividing East and West Berlin at the week-end.

Wrong side up . . . Firemen rescue driver K. Bell from his Vauxhall after it overturned at Cottage Corner during Saturday's saloon car race at Aintree.

Driver Bell was shaken but unhurt.

The saloon car race was held before the British Grand Prix.

TWISTWORDS

Find two words which mean the opposite of FIRM and LESS and rearrange the letters of the new words to give an eight-letter word meaning chief.

☐☐☐☐☐☐☐☐

Saturday's solution: The opposites were RAGE (calmness) and LEND (borrow). Twistword was ENLARGED.

36

At the Lotus headquarters in Cheshunt in 1963 and, opposite, preparing for the 1962 British Grand Prix, the last time it was held at Aintree

Clark takes a corner ahead of Dutchman Carel Godin de Beaufort on his way to victory in the 1962 British Grand Prix at Aintree

Clark with his friend and rival Graham Hill

Taking the chequered flag to
win the 1964 British Grand
Prix at Brands Hatch

WORLD CHAMPION DROVER!

Jim Clark finds one sheep-power as tough as 200 horse-power

The other world of Jim Clark . . . showing one of his sheep at Kelso yesterday.

THESE are the two faces of Jim. On the left is Jim Clark, farmer. On the right, Jim Clark, world champion racing driver.

Yesterday 27-year-old Jim forgot for a while about the world of spinning wheels and screaming exhausts.

He changed his crash-helmet for a tweed cap, his steering wheel for a shepherd's stick.

£2,000

Then he went to the sheep sales at Kelso, Roxburghshire—more a drover than a driver.

And the Flying Scot found that controlling a frisky ewe or ram—just one sheep-power—in the ring can be just as much trouble as keeping a sliding 200 horse-power racing car under control.

He and his father, who is also his partner, had forty-three sheep for sale. By the end of the day they were about £2,000 better off.

But today Jim will change the tweed cap for his crash helmet.

Jim Clark, world champion racing driver, is giving a demonstration at the Brands Hatch circuit in Kent.

Jim Clark . . . as the world of motor racing knows him.

BOUQUETS FOR YOUNG MUSICIANS

FRIDAY the Thirteenth was a day to remember for the National Youth Orchestra of Great Britain. These talented young musicians gave a concert in Zurich last night which sent the city's music-lovers into raptures.

It was the sixth concert in their tour of Poland and Switzerland, under Rudolf Schwarz.

Helen Powell, 16, of Milnthorpe, Westmorland, who played the solo in the Haydn Clarinet Concerto, was called back four times.

Today, the orchestra, sponsored by the Daily Mirror, will give the last concert of the tour

THE PHANTOM WHO RIDES AT MIDNIGHT

A PHANTOM Horseman rode through the English countryside yesterday.

And the scene that followed would have been a credit to any T V Western.

It had gunfire and the pounding of hooves from a suddenly-spurred horse.

It had a dramatic escape from death under the thundering wheels of a freight train.

The Phantom Horseman rode at Wombourn, Staffs, just after midnight. Earlier police from Willenhall kept watch following reports from farmers that wire fences had been cut and cattle driven out of fields.

They saw nothing.

Then Philip Westwood, 17, of Westwood Farm, stepped in.

He said last night: "I had a hunch that a phantom horseman might ride and at midnight on Thursday I noticed that field gates were open.

"I knocked up Will Ferrier, of Orton Grange. He brought his shotgun.

"Suddenly we saw a man on a grey horse who seemed to be driving cattle in one of Will's fields.

"I ran across and shouted: 'Get off!' Will fired his gun in the air, but the rider spurred his horse.

"I ran with him for fifty yards before he came to the railway track.

"He went across inches ahead of the steel train from Round Oak.

"He nearly killed himself and his horse. I phoned the police."

Yesterday Wombourn police said a man had been interviewed, but not detained. The matter was being referred to higher authority, they added.

All smiles after winning the
Martini Rossi title at
Snetterton in March 1963

Celebrating the second of his incredible feat of four successive British Grand Prix victories, this time at Silverstone in July 1963

Below:
Taking in some fuel of his own during the RAC Sun Rally of 1966
Right:
Receiving his trophy from Earl Mountbatten after winning the 1964 British Grand Prix at Brands Hatch

ONE of the most gifted natural racing talents to grace the F1 scene, Scotsman Clark was born into a farming family and always considered that to be his main calling.

After impressing in sprint meetings, his obvious talent saw a racing team, Border Reivers, set up with him in mind. After becoming the first driver to lap a post-war British circuit at over 100mph, he found himself competing with Colin Chapman, who duly signed him for the Lotus F2 team. Lotus would be the only team Clark raced for in his illustrious career.

He made his Formula One debut in the 1960 Dutch Grand Prix and after narrowly losing the 1962 World Drivers' Championship he clinched it the following year by winning seven of the 10 races. He won it again in 1965, when he also won the Indianapolis 500 in a Lotus 38, a first for a rear-engined car and the only time a driver won both titles in the same year.

After winning the first race of the 1968 season, Clark's life was tragically cut short, like so many of his contemporaries, when he crashed in a minor F2 race in Hockenheim. Lotus team-mate Graham Hill won the championship for the heartbroken team and duly dedicated the success to Clark.

The pictures on this page feature Clark before and during his fourth successive British Grand Prix triumph. This victory came in 1965 at Silverstone in his Lotus Climax

FACTFILE:
Born: Fife, 04.03.36.
Died: 07.04.68.
Teams: Lotus.
F1 wins: 25.
Podium positions: 32.
World championships: 2 (1963, 1965).
Pole positions: 33.
British GP wins: 5 (1962, 1963, 1964, 1965 and 1967).
First win: 1962 Belgian Grand Prix.
Last win: 1968 South African Grand Prix.

PAGE 4 DAILY MIRROR, Monday, September 8, 1969

The uncrowned king

Jackie Stewart's win in yesterday's Italian Grand Prix virtually makes him the 1969 World Champion. He's won 6 out of 8 Grands Prix this season, and taken second place in the German. All on Dunlop. And no-one knows better the difference a tyre can make.

Jackie Stewart doesn't win races with reckless heroics. He wins by brainwork, and hard intensive preparation. He's concerned with every engineering detail, and especially with tyres.

"The wrong tyre combination" he's said "can lose you as much as a second a lap on the corners. It could lose you the race."

At Dunlop we've been helping the Matra International racing team since 1968; helping them break lap records, drive through heat and downpour, stay ahead of the game with innovations like four-wheel-drive. We've sweated with Jackie and learnt a lot.

With each race, we're learning to make your tyres even better.

DUNLOP
Get Dunlop Confidence under you.

LABOUR QUIZ ON COUNCILS REVOLUTION

By DAVID THOMPSON

THE Labour Party launched a campaign yesterday to find out what its members think of plans for scrapping the present local government system.

It published a "discussion document" on the proposals.

And a series of regional conferences is to be held next month "to obtain the views of party members."

The proposals in question are those made earlier this year by the Redcliffe-Maud Commission on local government.

New

It recommended that there should be three big new metropolitan councils for Birmingham, Manchester and Liverpool, and fifty-eight powerful super-councils for the rest of England and Wales.

Above these super-councils would be eight provincial councils, and below them virtually powerless local councils.

The Labour document puts the commission's case, but suggests greater powers for the provincial councils and even smaller local councils than the commission proposes

Girl, 13, is attacked in castle cave

By RICHARD STOTT

A 13-YEAR-OLD girl was attacked and raped in a cave beneath ancient Hastings Castle yesterday.

The girl, who was playing among rocks below the castle, was dragged into the cave by a man who held her prisoner for twenty minutes.

Accent

Later police put out a TV and radio appeal for a man said to be about forty-five.

He spoke with a foreign accent and had a large, hooked nose.

Last night a police spokesman said: "The girl was not badly hurt but is very shaken by the ordeal."

Jackie Stewart, aged 17, with his first car, an Austin A35

With wife Helen before practice for the 1966 Monaco Grand Prix

Stewart is the centre of
attention after winning
the 1969 British Grand
Prix at Silverstone

49

TALKING
YESTERDAY—
THE WORLD
CHAMPION'S
WIFE..

Yes, it's fine for Jackie, but the race track's not for the children

WATCHING AND WAITING: Mrs. Helen Stewart with her sons Paul, 3, and Mark, 20 months.   PICTURE: Arthur Sidey.

from PAUL HUGHES
in Geneva

LITTLE Paul Stewart yelled "brmmm, brmmm" in imitation of a racing car as he rounded another bend on the drive of his home near Geneva in Switzerland.

Calmly his mother stood by and watched.

Golden-haired Mrs. Helen Stewart has grown used to watching and waiting. . . .

Her husband is Jackie Stewart, the 30-year-old Flying Scot who's sure to be this year's champion racing driver.

Return

While he's away Helen spends her time studiously relaxed, looking after their two sons Paul, three, and Mark, twenty months.

This time she'll have to wait until November for Jackie to return from races in America and Mexico.

*But Helen, from the little town of Helens-*burgh, *Dunbarton-shire, doesn't mind.*

"He will go on racing. It's his profession. It's what he wants to do—and it's not many men who are able to get paid to do something they enjoy," she said.

Raced

But as blond-haired Paul raced up and down the drive, Helen ruffled her younger son, Mark's, hair and added: "Yes, it's fine for Jackie, but the race track's not for the children.

"I don't want the boys to be racing drivers. I don't know whether I could stop them, but I certainly wouldn't encourage them. Jackie feels the same.

"*Racing is not a very safe profession. I would rather the children found something else to do.*"

But she admits that she could never change Jackie. And she wouldn't want to.

Thoughtfully, Helen, 28, turned the giant gold and diamond ring her husband had brought her from the States on a previous trip and said:

"Although Jackie has won the championship he will go on racing. They all do, all the drivers. When they've won one they want to win another, that's why they go on and on and on. . . .

"But that's what Jackie wants to do. And I'm his wife, and I'm quite happy about it."

Ran

Helen, daughter of a baker, met Jackie in the local teenage coffee bar when she was sixteen.

His parents ran a garage at Dumbuck, near Dumbarton. But because of his mother's disapproval Jackie did not start motor-racing seriously until after he was married, seven years ago.

Mrs. Stewart, her cool gaze flicking over the six acres of lawns and neatly trimmed shrubs overlooking the tidy Swiss landscape, said: "I like it here. Jackie's secretary Ruth is Scottish and we have a Scottish Nannie.

Relax

"And, of course, I have lots of friends who invite me out to dinner when Jackie is away racing.

"He tries to get home as often as possible but now he has more promotional work to do. . . .

"I think I would like to take a chalet up in the mountains somewhere in Switzerland and just relax in the peace and quiet.

"*It would make it easier while I'm waiting for Jackie.*"

50

With wife Helen and their two sons,
Paul and Mark

51

52

THE Flying Scot, Sir Jackie Stewart, helped bring in a new era of Formula One, campaigning vigorously for safety rules which undoubtedly saved the lives of many of his fellow competitors.

Stewart's first connection with cars came through his family's Jaguar dealership and watching older brother Jimmy compete. When Jimmy crashed at Le Mans, Jackie's parents encouraged him to take up another sport instead and he narrowly missed the cut for the 1960 Olympic clay pigeon shooting team.

After being persuaded by a customer to test some cars at Oulton Park, Jackie came to the attention of Ken Tyrrell who offered him an F3 drive in 1964. He switched to BRM and F1 in 1965, winning his first Grand Prix at Monza and being named Rookie of the Year in 1966.

A crash the same year in Belgium left him trapped in his car surrounded by leaking fuel and proved the catalyst for his tireless bid to see new safety measures introduced. He won the first of his three World Drivers' Championships in 1969, driving a Tyrrell-run Matra. Tyrrell built their own car from the following season, and with them and Cosworth, Stewart won the championship again in 1971 and 1973.

He won two British Grand Prix events at Silverstone in 1969 and 1971.

FACTFILE:
Born: Milton, 11.06.39.
Teams: BRM, Tyrrell.
F1 wins: 27.
Podium positions: 43.
World championships: 3
(1969, 1971, 1973).
Pole positions: 17.
British GP wins: 2
(1969, 1971).
First win: 1965 Italian GP.
Last win: 1973 German GP.

Left: Stewart lapped the entire field in his Matra on his way to winning the 1969 British Grand Prix. **Right:** With the Matra team in August 1969 and signing autographs in 1973. **Below:** Relaxing before the start of the 1970 British Grand Prix at Brands Hatch. On the opposite page, Stewart inspects instruments at a mobile hospital before a Grand Prix. He was a tireless and vociferous campaigner for improved safety standards

Daily Mirror

BRITAIN'S BIGGEST DAILY SALE

6p   Monday, October 25, 1976   No. 22,625

KING JAMES THE FIRST

The thirst of King James! Hunt races into a cooling can of Japanese beer.

BRITAIN'S James Hunt put his chequered past firmly behind him yesterday when he was crowned king of the world's racing drivers.

He gave an ice-cool display of driving in appalling conditions to finish third in the rain-hit Japanese Grand Prix—and take the title from Austria's Niki Lauda.

The victory came in true Hunt style. The race was packed with breathtaking incidents from start to finish. And the British "golden boy" was always in the thick of it.

At one stage it looked as if the jinx which has haunted him all season would rob him of glory.

He explained: "The front tyre started shredding, and I had rubbish all over my visor. I didnt know what the hell to do.

Convinced

"Then the tyre burst. I dropped some places during the pit stop, but I didn't know how many.

"At the finish I was convinced I still had to pass another couple of cars to regain third place. Fortunately, I was wrong."

Hunt's third place was just enough to give him a 69—68 points win over Lauda in the race to the championship.

Now Hunt, whose crashes once earned him the nickname "Shunt," can revel in his new title. King James.

Hunt's the raining champ

Poulson outburst by top judge

A ROCK-BOTTOM £... IT'S BUNK!

By ROBERT HEAD and JOHN DESBOROUGH

THE tipsters who talked about a deal to push down the value of the pound got it all wrong.

That was the message last night from the International Monetary Fund.

Britain wants a £2,300 million loan from the fund.

And a report in yesterday's Sunday Times claimed to detail the price we will have to pay.

The report said the IMF and the United States Treasury had agreed that there should be a sharp drop in the exchange rate of the pound.

The figure mentioned was a fall from 1.65 dollars to about 1.50 dollars.

A drop to 1.50 dollars would mean that the pound had been devalued by 26 per cent. since March.

And the suggestion seemed set to give t pound a hammering the exchange mark today.

The report received support in Briti Government circles y terday.

Then the IMF fi off its salvo.

IMF managing dir tor William Dale said Washington that story has "absolutely basis in fact."

DAILY MIRROR, Monday, October 25, 1976   PAGE 17

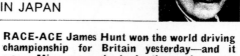

Fuji..where James Hunt finally buried his playboy image

he man from the Mirror,
the champion!

wait yesterday for the rain to stop—and the racing to start.

FROM
PATRICK MENNEM
IN JAPAN

RACE-ACE James Hunt won the world driving championship for Britain yesterday—and it was a Mirrorman who broke the good news to him.

Hunt, angry and confused, was standing in the McLaren pits after finishing third in the Japanese Grand Prix.

He was convinced he had finished fifth—and he needed to make third place to beat his arch-rival, Niki Lauda of Austria.

When I assured him he had come third, beating Lauda by one point, his face lit up and he threw his arms round a startled mechanic.

Team boss Teddy Mayer asked me: "Did we come third? Are you sure?"

"Yes," I said. "You're the champions."

No wonder they were confused after a day of high-speed drama on the glistening track.

Problems

The race started late, delayed by pelting rain which shrouded the road in mist and spray.

The first sensation came after only two laps, when Lauda's nerve cracked and he coasted his Ferrari into the pits.

Lauda, who almost died after crashing in the German Grand Prix in August, said brokenly: "It's too misty. Sometimes I couldn't tell which direction the car was going."

Out on the track, things were going well for Hunt.

He was confidently in the lead, and the rain had stopped. But the drying track brought its own problems . . .

Hunt's wet-weather tyres started to wear fast on the gritty surface. He slowed to nurse them—and lost the lead after holding it for 61 laps.

Patrick Depailler of France streaked past in his Elf Tyrell, then America's Mario Andretti took the lead in a John Player Special.

On lap 69 one of Hunt's front tyres burst, and he drew into the pits for a lightning wheel-change.

When he rejoined the race he believed he had fallen far behind. And four laps later, after receiving the chequered flag behind Andretti and Depailler, he arrived back at the pits furious.

"Why didn't you tell me to come in and change my tyres?" he screamed.

But it was all smiles and forgiveness when the Mirror broke the good news.

In clinching the world championship, he has at last buried the playboy image that has haunted him for years.

But there will be one small lapse, I can reveal. When I asked how he was going to celebrate last night he grinned and told me: "I'm going to get legless."

oar away.

MUM AND DAD BREAK OUT THE BUBBLY!

A FAMILY celebration was in full swing at the home of James Hunt's parents last night.

His mother, Mrs. Susan Hunt, said: "It's super to have a British world champion, and we're all very proud of him."

This morning Mr. and Mrs. Hunt left home in Belmont, Surrey, with three of their five children to watch the race live at a television studio.

Mrs. Hunt added: "The last laps were nail-biting. I spoke to James after the race and he's fine."

James's 78-year-old grandmother, Mrs. Barbara Davis, said: "I'm on top of the world. I couldn't be happier."

PROUD: James's parents

SUZIE: Thrilled.

'He got what he wanted'

JAMES HUNT'S lovely ex-wife Suzie had a message of congratulations for the new champ yesterday.

She told a friend she was "thrilled for James, and pleased he got what he wanted."

Suzie, 27, is in Arizona with her new husband, Richard Burton, who is working on a film.

It was in February this year that rumours first started of a break-up between James and Suzie, a former model.

She obtained a "quickie" divorce, and married Burton in August.

Proud

Another of James's well-wishers was millionaire Lord Hesketh, whose own racing team broke up just before the start of this season.

Lord Hesketh, who had James as his number one driver, said: "I spent £750,000 and people said I was mad.

"But I don't begrudge James anything. He's one of the few people in Britain we can be proud of."

"My only regret is that we didn't win the championship together.

"But James didn't leave until we could no longer afford to go on."

POULSON AND MP: A JUDGE HITS OUT

By JOHN DESBOROUGH and ROGER TODD

ATTORNEY-GENERAL Sam Silkin was criticised last night for failing to take action over a letter sent by an MP to architect John Poulson.

The criticism came from Lord Salmon, a Lord of Appeal, and chairman of last year's inquiry into standards of conduct in public life.

He spoke out after the letter was published in The Observer yesterday.

The letter, dated March 2, 1965, was from John Cordle, Tory MP for Bournemouth East.

Mr. Cordle suggested in it that he should have received more than £150 for helping Poulson.

The MP wrote: "It was largely for the benefit of Construction Promotion [a Poulson firm] that I took part in a debate in the House of Commons. . . ."

The letter was seen by the bankruptcy court which dealt with Poulson before he was jailed for corruption.

Aware

It was referred to Lord Salmon's Royal Commission in January last year.

Lord Salmon said last night: "MPs in general were not aware of its existence.

"But the Attorney-General and other Ministers were aware of the letter.

"Mr. Silkin and I spoke about it.

"That is why I am surprised that nothing has been done to refer the letter to the Commons Committee of Privileges which could take action."

The Privileges Committee deals, among other things, with allegations about MPs' conduct.

It has wide powers to recommend punishment for anyone who appears before it.

Duties

The penalties can include expulsion from the House.

Last week Premier James Callaghan announced that the Commons would be asked to set up a high-powered select committee to probe allegations about MPs being involved with Poulson in respect of their Parliamentary duties.

The terms of the inquiry and the committee's membership will be discussed this week.

On BBC Radio yesterday, Lord Salmon said he did not know how far the investigation would go.

He added: "All one can criticise is the fact that it was thought that this letter was not deserving of being referred to the

The letter to Poulson

EXTRACTS from Mr. Cordle's letter to John Poulson:

Dear John . . .

It was largely for the benefit of Construction Promotion that I took part in a debate in the House of Commons on the Gambia and pressed for H.M.G. to award construction contracts to British firms . . .

I have advocated that you should . . . be appointed consultant architect to the Gambian Government . . .

Having been elected Chairman of the Anglo-Libyan Group in the House of Commons I was in a good position to give Construction Promotion the right contacts . . .

May I remind you that I was encouraged . . . when at your office you said that a cheque was to be paid to me of some substance . . . I feel that the expenses cheque so far paid of £150 is somewhat uncomplimentary to myself . . .

On three occasions I personally saw Ministers of the Crown on behalf of Construction Promotion, Mr. James Callaghan, the chancellor, Sir Keith Joseph, and Mr. D. Jay, President of the Board of Trade.

Yours Sincerely,
John Cordle

Committee of Privileges."

Mr. Cordle has said he has done nothing to be ashamed of.

Support for him came yesterday from Mrs. Kathleen Palmer, chairman of Bournemouth East Conservative Association.

She said: "He wouldn't try to take money to which he is not entitled.

"I'm sure he will remain our MP. I was with him last night at a social function and he warned me to expect 'hell' again."

The win that never was: Celebrating victory in the controversial 1976 British Grand Prix at Brands Hatch. Two months after the race, Hunt was disqualified following a protest by Ferrari and Niki Lauda declared winner

In action in his McLaren number one car in the Race of Champions at Brands Hatch in 1977

Fully focused as he prepares
for action in 1976

On holiday in Spain in 1975

Jogging on a Marbella beach
with his pet dog in 1979

61

At the wheel again in 1982, but this time a tractor is his mode of transporation

62

Receiving a lift from some of his legion of female fans at the 1976 British Grand Prix

With another star of British motorsport from the 1970s, motorcyclist Barry Sheene and Sheene's future wife Stephanie McLean

After his disqualification in 1976, Hunt won the British Grand Prix at Silverstone a year later

'HUNT the Shunt' epitomised the glamorous lifestyle many associate with Formula One. During his racing career he was associated with a bevy of beauties and wore a badge on his overalls which read: 'Sex – Breakfast of Champions.'

Behind the playboy image was a racing driver of immense talent. Hunt started by competing in a homebuilt Mini racer before graduating to Formula Ford and F3. In 1973 he joined the Hesketh F1 team, racing in an unsponsored car and managing an excellent win in the 1975 Dutch Grand Prix before money ran out.

Desperate for a drive, Hunt signed for McLaren for the 1976 season and it would prove quite a year. He was disqualified and then reinstated as winner of the Spanish Grand Prix, stripped of the British win and forced to start from the back of the grid in Italy. However, he still won six races and by the final race in Japan was only three points behind Niki Lauda. Torrential rain led to Lauda's retirement and, despite a puncture, Hunt paddled his way to third position, enough to take the world championship.

In 1978, Hunt heroically dragged Ronnie Peterson from a burning car at Monza but his friend later died of his injuries. Disheartened, Hunt retired in 1979 and never raced again. He started work as a BBC commentator in 1980, a role he filled until his death from a heart attack in 1993.

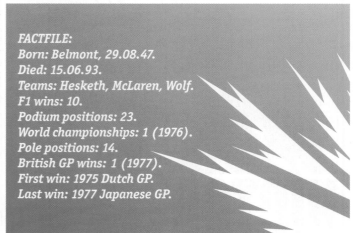

FACTFILE:
Born: Belmont, 29.08.47.
Died: 15.06.93.
Teams: Hesketh, McLaren, Wolf.
F1 wins: 10.
Podium positions: 23.
World championships: 1 (1976).
Pole positions: 14.
British GP wins: 1 (1977).
First win: 1975 Dutch GP.
Last win: 1977 Japanese GP.

NIGEL MANSELL

FANZINE TRIBUTE TO THE WORLD'S GREATEST RACING DRIVER FANZINE

NIGEL'S INDY-STRUCTIBLE!

ONE FOR THE ROAD
NIGEL Mansell had a few last-minute technical problems to ponder before his first IndyCar race — but whatever he thought up here, it certainly worked.

A five star show by Mansell

From TED MACAULEY in Surfers Paradise, Australia

RIP-ROARING record buster Nigel Mansell waved the flag for Britain with that old familiar High Five yesterday.

That's the race number he carried to Formula One Grand Prix glory. Now, the number five is emblazoned in the record books again.

This time, the £8million-a-year Brummie, is doing his stuff in IndyCar racing — and he's on course for the title.

His team bosses, Hollywood superstar Paul Newman and Chicago businessman Carl Haas, paid £300,000 to buy the number five from a rival Indy runner.

"We wanted to make Nigel feel at home," said Newman. "The number was good for him when it was red five in Formula One and maybe it'll be the same in our Indy series.

He daily won — by five seconds. But Florida-based Mansell needed all the luck he could get to go with his daring as he skirted disaster in front of 100,000 sunbaked fans.

Mansell insists has gripped Australia just as strongly as it did Europe. And now it looks as if his anonymity in America will be blasted aside.

"Yes, it looks as if all that privacy I've treasured will disappear. My face will be a bit better known now having won my first Indy race," he said.

On pole after setting a lap record during the qualifying season, Mansell became the first rookie driver to win his first Indy race since the late Graham Hill won the Indianapolis 500 in 1966.

It was also the 1992 Formula One champion's first victory on Australian soil. "I can't remember the last time I enjoyed racing like that," a jubilant Mansell told reporters.

It took him an hour to make it 300 yards from the finish line through the mob of wellwishers to find his wife Rosanne for a hugs-and-kisses celebration.

And more than 90 countries saw his breathtaking Indy breakthrough on television.

He didn't even realise — or care that he had won a bonus of £20,600 for the fastest lap and pole position.

His amazing victory first tipped out in Indy overshadowed the small change. And his only celebration drink was a litre of milkshake to wash down his roast lamb dinner.

"Let's try to keep it in perspective," he said. "The win is great, it's fabulous and I'm chuffed ... but there's a long way to go yet."

INSURANCE GROUP

EVERYTHING'S ROSY
NIGEL's wife Rosanne helps him celebrate his brilliant IndyCar success in Australia

A FIVE, A FIVE-OH
THAT famous number five is back on Nigel Mansell's car — and he showed all the old Formula One style to leave the others trailing

THE FIRST OF MANY
The race is won — and Nigel Mansell

DAILY Mirror

GAME CARD INSIDE TODAY
Michael Jackson LIVE
WIN PEPSI
TICKETS TO SEE HIM IN PARIS LONDON BARCELONA

Monday, July 13, 1992 NEWSPAPER FOR THE NINETIES Last month's daily sale 3,596,544 (INCORPORATING THE DAILY RECORD) 25p

CRY

VICTORY

Fans go wild for Mansell

By MARTIN PHILLIPS

THIS is the moment when it all became too much for race hero Nigel Mansell.

The tough-guy of the track wept with emotion after being crowned King of British motor racing.

Mansell thrilled 300,000 screaming fans as he scorched his way into the record books with a 36th Grand Prix victory.

Wiping away the tears, he said: "It's the most wonderful day of my life." The true Brit punched the air

Picture by ARNOLD SLATER

MIRROR SPORT

MANSELL MANIA

Nigel is mobbed

By TED MACAULEY

GRAND PRIX hero Nigel Mansell was mobbed by a delirious crowd of 200,000 at Silverstone yesterday.

The sky-speed Brummie had to be pulled clear by a rescue squad of police and marshalls.

They all wanted a piece of the great man after his runaway victory in the British Grand Prix, and the conquering Renault-Williams was raided for souvenir pieces as Mansell fled to the safety of his motorhome.

Later, he yelled to the crowd through a microphone: "This win is for you all. I dedicate it to you."

Mansell said: "That was the greatest race of my career and the greatest lap in the history of British motor racing. I dedicate this victory to the fans, who were completely amazing today.

"I've never experienced anything like that in all of my career and have never seen anything like it in the world. The fans were everywhere."

In an never-to-be-forgotten afternoon, the £8million-a-year superstar blazed a breathtaking trail of glory ...

● He won by a massive margin of nearly 40 seconds.
● He blasted the lap record to smithereens.
● He became the most successful British Grand Prix driver of all time.

You can read my paper now, I've finished.

GUINNESS

PURE GENIUS.

HERO
FANTASTIC: Nigel Mansell, hero of Silverstone, salutes an epic victory yesterday.

Published by MGN Ltd, at 22 Holborn, London EC1P 1DQ (071-353 0246) and printed by Mirror Colour Print Ltd, in Watford. Registered as a newspaper at the Post Office. Serial No. 35743 Thirsday, tel, 1992, Monday, July 13, 1992

9 770950 605110
29

MIRROR SPORT

THE FANS GO WILD

BRITAIN LOVES YOU NIGEL!

MOBBED

MANSELL is deluged by jubilant fans.

ONE IN THE EYE

By BRYAN RIMMER

MAGNIFICENT Nigel Mansell yesterday paid tribute to the crowd that roared him to glory in the British Grand Prix.

The sensation of Silverstone said he owed his third successive Grand Prix victory in Britain to the record 120,000 fans who willed him home.

Mansell was mobbed by them as he tried to finish his victory lap and he said: "They were magnificent. I was driving with crowd-power — I reckon they put five seconds in my pocket. They won the race for me.

HERO

Nigel Mansell celebrates in champagne style after his brilliant win in the British Grand Prix at Silverstone yesterday.

"As I chased Nelson I could see them waving and willing me on. They helped tremendously."

Mansell even played down the bitter rivalry between the two Williams' drivers which had led to the event being dubbed the "Race of Hate."

He said: "Nelson drove brilliantly. If he had stopped to change tyres as I did he would have won the race.

Grand show

"But my own change of tyres gave me victory. I had much better grip and handling than earlier in the race."

"It turned out to be the fastest race I've ever driven with an average speed of over 146 mph."

Mansell also revealed how perilously close he came to losing.

He said: "I came the closest I've ever been to running out of fuel. The car started spluttering and coughing on the slow-down lap. I daren't tell you what the dashboard was reading."

Published by Mirror Group Newspapers (1986) Ltd. (01-353 0246) and printed by British Newspaper Printing Corporation (London) Ltd., Holborn Circus, London EC1P 1DQ. Registered at the Post Office as a newspaper.   Serial No. 26,926 © The Daily Mirror Newspapers, Ltd., 1987

Clockwise from above:
How the Mirror reported Nigel Mansell's British Grand Prix wins of 1987 and 1992, plus his debut success in IndyCar in 1993

Before, during and after the 1992 British Grand Prix at Silverstone, when Mansell was mobbed by delirious fans. He was crowned world champion a month later

In pensive mood at the 1990 Silverstone race when he was a Ferrari driver

72

The frustration shows after Mansell was forced to retire from the 1990 British Grand Prix. Immediately after the race, he announced he would leave F1 at the end of that season, only to change his mind and re-sign for Williams

WHEN a young Nigel Mansell suffered a broken neck following a crash in testing at Brands Hatch during the 1970s, doctors told him he would never drive again. Mansell simply discharged himself from hospital and went on to win the 1977 Formula Ford Championship.

Such was his determination to succeed that he and wife Rosanne sold their house to finance a 1979 move into Formula Three. The gamble paid off and earned him a job as Lotus test driver with three F1 starts in 1980.

Following four frustrating years playing second fiddle to Elio De Angelis, Mansell signed for Williams in 1985 and was installed in the 'Red Five' car he would make famous.

Brands Hatch, the scene of the crash that had almost left him paralysed, became the stage for his first F1 success when he took the chequered flag in the European

Grand Prix. Runner-up, heartbreakingly, to Alain Prost and then Nelson Piquet in the World Drivers' Championship in 1986 and 1987 respectively, he had two seasons at Ferrari in 1989 and 1990 but still the title evaded him.

He returned to Williams in 1991 and had another near miss in his quest for the championship but in 1992, his perseverance paid off as millions of Britons tuned in to the Hungarian Grand Prix to see a second-place finish provide confirmation of his long-awaited success.

After leaving F1 to try his luck in the CART IndyCar World Series, he won the 1993 championship with the Newman/Haas team – becoming the only driver to hold both titles simultaneously.

Hugely popular with the public, Mansell also won the BBC Sports Personality of the Year award twice, in 1986 and 1992 – one of only three people to do so.

Ready to leave the pits in his Williams, while, below, he gives team-mate Alain Prost a lift in 1990

FACTFILE:
Born: Upton-upon-Severn, 08.08.53.
Teams: Lotus, Williams, Ferrari, McLaren.
F1 wins: 31.
Podium positions: 59.
World championships: 1 (1992).
Pole positions: 32.
British GP wins: 4 (1986, 1987, 1991, 1992).
First win: 1985 European Grand Prix (Brands Hatch).
Last win: 1994 Australian Grand Prix.

OWN ONE OF THE MOST DRAMATIC GRAND PRIX PICTURES OF ALL TIME

Buy this classic Graham Hill image as an A2 or A3 framed print

Framed A2 print 420mm x 594mm · £99.99 inclusive delivery
Framed A3 print 297mm x 429mm · £59.99 inclusive delivery

Postal/Cheques orders to: Mirrorpix, 22nd Floor, One Canada Square, Canary Wharf,
London, E14 5AP. Cheques made payable to: Mirrorpix. Or Call 020 7293 3740

MIRROR SPORT SALUTES A TRUE BRIT HERO

HILL-verstone

FLYING THE FLAG: Damon Hill raises the Union Jack during his triumphant victory lap at Silverstone yesterday

This is the best day of my life

**Words: Ted Macauley
Pictures: Dale Cherry**

DAMON HILL woke up in his hotel room yesterday morning and vowed: "I'm going to win the British Grand Prix."

He was as good as his word as Silverstone became Hill-verstone with 80,000 fans cheering him to the echo as he held aloft the trophy he most wanted to win.

He roared: "There have been some great names on it, and I'm proud to join them.

Family

"My dad Graham never managed to win it — and now I feel I have filled in a little bit of a hole in our family achievements."

The 33-year-old Londoner, currently second in the world championship had a massive title boost after his victory, and was close to tears.

He said: "I feel absolutely terrific. This is the best day of my life. It's like a dream. I don't want it to end.

"I feel it is destiny — and that my name was written on this trophy."

Hill, who raged away from a press conference in anger four days ago after it was suggested his Rothmans-Williams job was under threat, added: "I don't want to talk about any of that. I just want to enjoy this fantastic day . . . this fantastic day — the best day of my life.

"I just feel that everything in my life has suddenly come together at this point.

"And I feel as if I was destined to win this race."

He didn't care that he was handed a big chance when Michael Schumacher was hit by a stop-go black-flag penalty and said: "Even if Michael hadn't had the penalty I still think I would have won.

"I knew I would have had to have pushed quite hard because he would be pretty hyped up.

Challenge

"I didn't know why he had been penalised — but it was a bit of a Godsend.

"But honestly, when I woke up this morning I knew that I could win. All I had to do was give it my best shot.

"I felt the car was good — and I felt I was ready for the challenge."

GOLD TOP: Silverstone king Hill plants a smacker on the trophy

Herr they go!

MIGHTY Germany are heading home after being humbled in New York's Giants Stadium yesterday.

In one of the biggest upsets in World Cup history the reigning champions were reduced to mere mortals by outsiders Bulgaria in a stunning 2-1 quarter-final defeat.

The result hands the Bulgarians a semi-final clash with Italy and turned the form book upside down.

Before this World Cup, Bulgaria had failed to win a single match in 16 attempts, while three-times champions Germany have been in four of the last five finals.

The Bulgarians even came from behind to win, having conceded a dubious penalty following a challenge on Juergen Klinsmann.

German skipper Lothar Matthaus scored from the spot – but Bulgaria hit back with two superb goals in three minutes from Hristo Stoichkov and Yordan Lechkov.

Sweden beat Romania in a penalty shoot-out to face Brazil in the other semi-final on Wednesday.

MATCH REPORTS - Pages 34, 35

£5M Chase on for Chris

By RICHARD TANNER

NORWICH last night triggered British soccer's biggest auction when they put Chris Sutton up for sale for a massive £5million – then insisted the cash must be in their bank by Friday!

And Carrow Road chairman Robert Chase also demanded that his club

9 770956 805219

Above:
Colliding with arch rival Michael Schumacher while battling for the lead in the 1995 British Grand Prix, while, below, he spins off from the 1996 race. On the opposite page Hill is shown on the day he signed for Williams in 1992, and testing his father's 'Hill GH2' F1 car in 1987

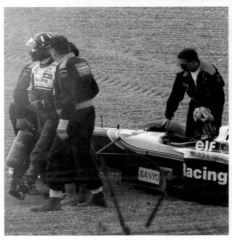

DESPITE having a former world champion for a father, Damon Hill refused to trade on his dad Graham's name as he went about making his own way in motorsport.

Starting out as a motorcycle racer, Hill made the switch to four wheels in 1984, working as a dispatch rider to finance his efforts.

After cutting his teeth in Formula Ford, F3 and F3000, he made his F1 debut with Brabham, managing to qualify in a couple of mid-season races in 1992. He was also testing for Williams at the time and, on the surprise departure of Nigel Mansell, Hill was promoted to partner Alain Prost in 1993. The following year his team-mate was Ayrton Senna until the Brazilian's tragic death at Imola.

Twenty-six years earlier, Graham Hill had won the world title for Lotus after the

death of team-mate Jim Clark and Damon almost did the same for Williams, only to be pipped by Michael Schumacher following a controversial collision with his German rival at the Australian Grand Prix.

After a disappointing 1995 season, Hill hit top form in 1996, winning eight races on his way to an excellent championship win which saw him finish 19 points clear of his nearest rival, Jacques Villeneuve.

He was also voted BBC Sports Personality of the Year for 1996, joining boxer Henry Cooper and Nigel Mansell as the only men to win the award twice.

Damon and father Graham are the only father and son to have been crowned F1 world champions.

Clockwise from left:
Celebrating his World Championship win at Marble Arch in 1996, concentrating hard at the 1994 British Grand Prix and preparing to play guitar at his Jordan team's post-race party in 1999. On the opposite page, Hill waves to the crowd after finishing sixth at Silverstone in 1997

FACTFILE:
Born: Hampstead, 17.09.60.
Teams: Brabham, Williams, Arrows, Jordan.
F1 wins: 22.
Podium positions: 42.
World championships: 1 (1996).
Pole positions: 20.
British GP wins: 1 (1994).
First win: 1993 Hungarian Grand Prix.
Last win: 1998 Belgian Grand Prix.

LEWIS HAMILTON

HAMILTON IS WORLD CHAMPION | **HE CLINCHES** | **TITLE IN MOST DRAMATIC OF CIRCUMSTANCES**

Finishing fifth has never felt so GOOD

LAST-CORNER HEROICS GIVE LEWIS THE CROWN

TEARS AS MASSA LOSES IT

HOW LEWIS SNATCHED IT

PHEW.. LEW HAS DONE IT

YOUNGEST IN HISTORY

Good luck, son: A hug from father Anthony before the 2007 British Grand Prix at Silverstone. Hamilton finished third

LEWIS HAMILTON'S fairytale rise to F1 world champion began when he started racing go-karts at the age of eight.

When he was 10 he met Ron Dennis, the owner and director of the McLaren Formula 1 team and told him he wanted to race in F1. At 13, he was signed up on the McLaren young driver programme and the team gave him the support he needed to achieve his dream.

As a youngster, he won several karting series, including the European Formula A Championship in 2000. After a year in Formula Renault, he won the 2003 British Formula Renault championship with 10 victories. In 2005, he won the F3 Euroseries and in 2006 took the GP2 title in his first season.

Moving up to Formula One in 2007, his remarkable rise continued. Hamilton finished third in his first race and proceeded to smash the 40-year-old rookie record of two consecutive podiums at the start of a season. He went on to achieve nine podiums in his first nine races, winning two of them. In total, he won four Grand Prix in 2007, finishing his debut season as runner-up in the World Drivers' Championship, just one point behind the winner, Ferrari's Kimi Raikkonen. It was the best season by a rookie driver in the sport.

In 2008, he realised the potential he had shown by going one better to become the youngest ever world champion. He needed to finish in the top five in the final race of the season in Brazil to achieve the feat, leaving it until the very last corner to overtake German driver Timo Glock and achieve the placing he required.

FACTFILE:
Born: Hampstead, 07.01.85.
Teams: McLaren.
F1 wins: 9.
Podium positions: 22.
World championships: 1
(2008).
Pole positions: 13.

British GP wins: 1 (2008).
First win: 2007 Canadian GP.
Last win: 2008 Chinese GP.

* Stats correct up to and
including 29.05.09.

Mirror Sport
mirrorsport@mgn.co.uk
28 pages today

FERGIE & BECKS
The untold story
EXCLUSIVE: PAGES 60 & 61

QUINN PEEKS

INSIDE
IT'S BACK!
YOUR No.1
PULL-OUT

After 113 races, 6½ years
17,681 miles, 5,836 laps..

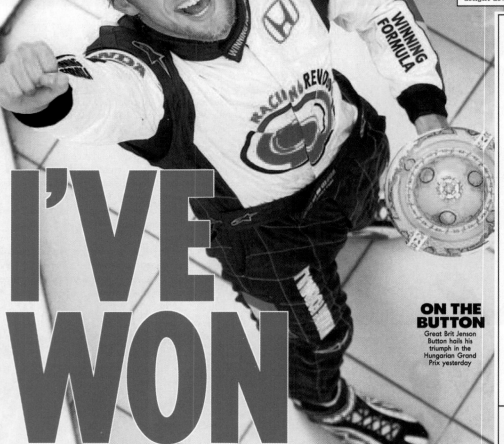

From BYRON YOUNG in Budapest

JENSON BUTTON stood on top of the world last night after finally silencing the doubters to land his first Formula One win.

The 26-year-old was losing his voice after screaming in delight down the team radio over the final laps of a dramatic day in Hungary.

The Honda driver ended an agonising six-and-half-year wait for his maiden victory with a remarkable drive after starting 14th on the grid.

"Wow, what a day," said Button. "To come from 14th to win is just fantastic. We

I'VE WON

ON THE BUTTON
Great Brit Jenson Button hails his triumph in the Hungarian Grand Prix yesterday

Published by MGN Ltd. at One Canada Square, Canary Wharf, London, E14 5AP (020-7293 3000) and printed by Trinity Mirror Printing Ltd. at Watford, Oldham and Birmingham. Registered as a newspaper at the Post Office. **Serial No. 32,800** ©MGN Ltd. Monday, August 7, 2006 ■ ■ ■ ■ ■ ■ ■ ■ ★★★ Austria 3.00EUR, Belgium 2.00 EUR, France 2.00 EUR, Germany 2.00 EUR, Greece 2.00 EUR, Italy 2.00 EUR, Netherlands 2.00 EUR, Portugal 2.00 EUR (continent) 341Esc, Spain 2.00EUR, Malta 53 cents, Turkey: 5.50YTL, Cyprus £1.05, Denmark 20DK

NEWSPAPERS SUPPORT RECYCLING
Recycled paper made up 80.3% of the raw material for UK newspapers in 2005